Moving

by Vana Dougias

PEARSON

Scott Foresman

Editorial Offices: Glenview, Illinois • Parsippany, New Jersey • New York, New York
Sales Offices: Needham, Massachusetts • Duluth, Georgia • Glenview, Illinois
Coppell, Texas • Ontario, California • Mesa, Arizona

Every effort has been made to secure permission and provide appropriate credit for photographic material. The publisher deeply regrets any omission and pledges to correct errors called to its attention in subsequent editions.

Unless otherwise acknowledged, all photographs are the property of Scott Foresman, a division of Pearson Education.

Photo locators denoted as follows: Top (T), Center (C), Bottom (B), Left (L), Right (R), Background (Bkgd)

Cover ©Ariel Skelley/Corbis; 1 ©Tony Arruza/Corbis; 3 ©James Marshall/Corbis; 5 ©Charles O'Rear/Corbis; 6 ©Joel W. Rogers/Corbis; 7 ©Images.com/Corbis; 9 ©Ariel Skelley/Corbis; 10 ©Chris North; Cordaiy Photo Library Ltd./Corbis; 12 ©Bob Krist/Corbis; 15 ©Jose Fuste Raga/Corbis; 17 ©Tony Arruza/Corbis; 19 ©Thinkstock; 21 ©Wolfgang Kaehler/Corbis; 22 ©Staffan Widstrand/Corbis; 24 ©Owen Franken/Corbis

ISBN: 0-328-13556-9

The first time my family and I moved I was just three years old. I was born in Boston, Massachusetts. We lived there before my dad got a new job in California. Even though I was only three when we moved, I remember a few things about Boston. My mom used to take my big sister, Sarah, and me, Joey, to the park.

At the park, we fed the ducks and the pigeons. Sometimes we would go for a ride on the swan boats. Because I was so young when we left, I don't remember much more about the city. I do remember the park, though. It was my favorite place.

Because of my dad's job, we have moved around a lot. I'm only twelve years old, and I've already lived in five places. Moving so much has been tough. It can be hard getting used to new places and making new friends, and it is hard to say good-bye to the friends you leave behind. There are good things about moving, too. My sister and I have learned a lot about different people and different places, and now we both have friends all over the world!

My dad works for an engineering firm with projects all over the world. So he has to go where the company needs him. Luckily, my mom is a writer for a magazine, and she is able to work from home.

Not only is she a great writer, but she is also an amazing person who is always there for us. She and my dad have been a big help to my sister and me. They know how hard it can be to adjust to a new environment.

Moving to San Francisco was really exciting for all of us. My mom and dad were both familiar with the city because they grew up nearby. My mom was born in Fresno, and my dad grew up in Oakland, which is just across the bay from San Francisco. By coincidence, they both attended college in Boston. That is where they met and got married.

After they graduated from college, my mom and dad decided to stay in Boston for a while. They both got jobs there. They thought it would be a great place to raise a family. A few years later, my sister and I were born. Boston became our first home.

Our second home was in San Francisco, on the west coast of the United States, over three-thousand miles away from Boston. Like Boston, San Francisco, is right on the ocean. Boston is a port city on the Atlantic Ocean, and San Francisco is a port city on the Pacific Ocean. The two cities have a lot of similarities, but there are also many differences between them. For one thing, it gets a lot colder in Boston!

Pacific Ocean

3,179 miles

San Francisco

Since I was older when we were in San Francisco, I have more memories of what it was like to live there. As I mentioned before, it doesn't get as cold in San Francisco as it does in Boston, but it does get really foggy. San Francisco is also a very hilly place.

My mom would take us on walks through the winding, steep streets of our neighborhood, and when we got to the top of a hill, we would turn around and look out at the bright blue Pacific Ocean. We also took a lot of drives along the coast on the weekends. Our parents brought us to Oakland and Fresno many times to see where they grew up and to visit our grandparents.

Boston

e United States

Atlantic Ocean

We lived in San Francisco for two years. I had just turned five and was supposed to start kindergarten in the fall. My sister was seven years old and had just finished the first grade. Then our parents told us the news. We were moving again.

Because I had not started school yet, the idea of moving was not so hard for me to accept. My sister became very upset, however. She cried because she loved her school and didn't want to leave her friends. My mother gave her a hug. She assured my sister that—although it would be hard at first— she would like her new school just as much. She explained that it is always hard to leave the places and people you know for something unknown.

"Is it hard for you and Dad to move from place to place?" I asked.

"Of course it is, Joey. We have a hard time leaving our friends and family behind, too. Also, we know that moving is hard on you and your sister," Mom said.

It turned out that the next place we moved to was in a different country! My dad's engineering firm was opening up a new office in London, England. We only had a few weeks to pack up all of our things and say good-bye to our friends and family. I was going to miss our walks through the hilly streets and all of the other fun things we did while we were in San Francisco.

Not only would we miss our friends and family, but my sister and I were scared about moving to a different country. Although people in England and the United States speak the same language, we were worried that we wouldn't understand the customs of another country.

I started to get really scared when I realized I would have to start school in England! What if I couldn't understand what the other kids were saying? What if they couldn't understand me? What if I have a hard time with my schoolwork? By the time we got to our new apartment in London, I was so nervous I could hardly eat. I began to understand why my sister was so upset.

On the morning of our first day of school in London, I was feeling a combination of fear and excitement. I had a tough time eating my cereal at breakfast because my stomach was tied up in knots. Luckily, my mother promised to take my sister and me to school. She wanted to make sure that we felt safe and secure.

I remember this day especially well because it was the first time we rode on the London Underground. The Underground is the system of subway trains that run beneath London. If you have ever been to a city with a subway system, then you know what I mean.

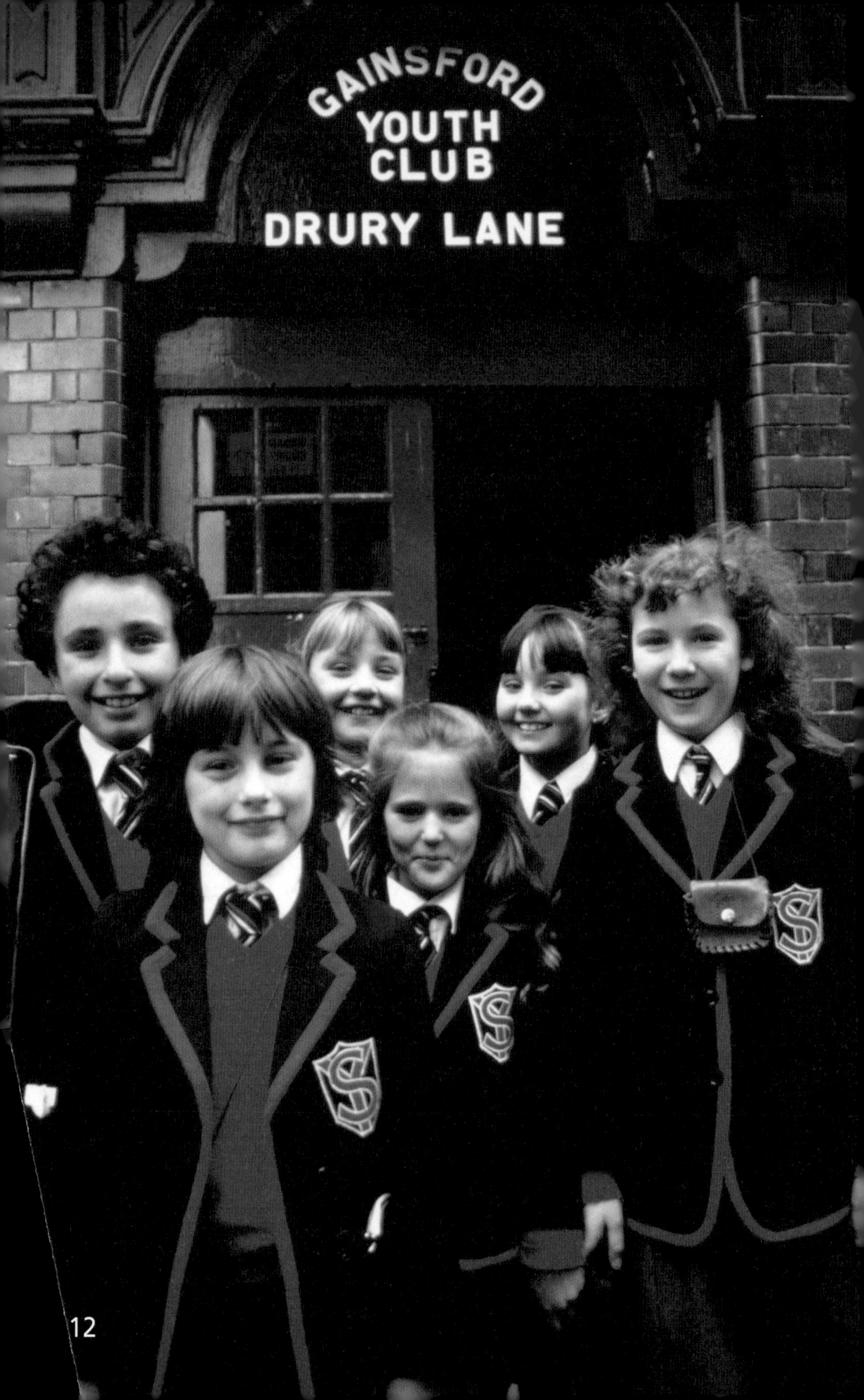
GAINSFORD
YOUTH
CLUB
DRURY LANE

The underground train is called "the Tube" by people who live in London. Many people ride the Tube to and from work and school every day. I remember very clearly when the train rushed into the station and the doors opened. A voice coming through a speaker told us to, "Mind the gap," and I asked my mom what that meant. She explained that it meant we should watch our step when entering the train. There was a gap between the train and the platform, and you had to be careful to step over it.

"Why don't they just say, 'Watch your step?'" I asked.

"They say things differently here than in the United States, honey," said my mom.

She wasn't kidding. In the two years that we lived in London, I learned that there are many differences in the way the British and Americans speak. I was worried that no one in England would like me because I was different. I was worried that the rules of my new school would be very strict and that I wouldn't understand what I was supposed to do.

I was so nervous on my first day of school that I became very quiet. I am always a little shy when I first meet someone or when I am in a new situation. Usually, once I get to know a person or place, I start to relax and be myself. My mom says everyone goes through that at first. She said I shouldn't worry too much about it. It always takes time to feel comfortable in a new place, she told me.

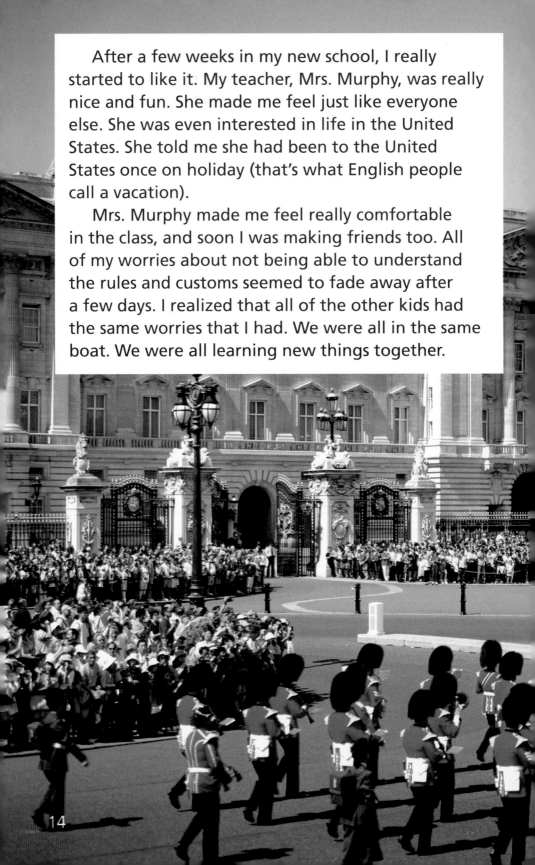

After a few weeks in my new school, I really started to like it. My teacher, Mrs. Murphy, was really nice and fun. She made me feel just like everyone else. She was even interested in life in the United States. She told me she had been to the United States once on holiday (that's what English people call a vacation).

Mrs. Murphy made me feel really comfortable in the class, and soon I was making friends too. All of my worries about not being able to understand the rules and customs seemed to fade away after a few days. I realized that all of the other kids had the same worries that I had. We were all in the same boat. We were all learning new things together.

We lived in London for two years, and in that time both my sister and I made a lot of new friends. It turns out my sister really did learn to like her new school as much as she had liked the old one. She made new friends in London, and she kept in touch with friends back in California.

I made a lot of new friends in London, too. My best friend's name was Jarvis. Jarvis and I both really love to play soccer (soccer is called football in England) and that's how we first started talking to each other. Jarvis taught me a lot about English sports like cricket and rugby.

I still keep in touch with Jarvis, even though we haven't seen each other since my family moved away from London. We send e-mails to each other just about every week. He keeps me up-to-date on our friends and sends me the latest soccer scores. I write him about my new friends and my new soccer team. I sent him a digital picture of me in the dentist's chair, getting my cavities filled! Sometimes we even write actual letters. Sending a letter overseas is really cool because you can use special airmail paper.

It's good to keep in touch with old friends. It makes moving to a new place a lot easier to handle. Knowing that you have friends allows you to relax when you're in a new place. Moving is always stressful, but there are things you can do to make it easier.

One of the best things you can do when you move to a new place is get involved in an activity or club that interests you. My sister and I both play soccer, so we have made a lot of friends by joining a game at recess and by joining teams or clubs. My sister also plays the violin, so she meets a lot of people who are into music. I don't play an instrument myself, but I do have other interests.

YUKON
TERRITORY

NORTHERN
TERRITORIES

NEWFOUNDLAND

BRITISH
COLUMBIA

ALBERTA

MANITOBA

QUEBEC

SASKATCHEWAN

ONTARIO

NEW
BRUNSWICK

NOVA
SCOTIA

Toronto

I like to read a lot, and I also like to watch television and movies. When we moved for the third time—to the city of Toronto, in Canada—I realized that I had a lot in common with Canadian kids my age. For example, I would mention an episode of my favorite television show, and a lot of the other kids liked the same show.

By the time we moved to Canada, I was eight years old and going into the third grade. It didn't take me long to make friends in Toronto because of something very important that I realized—a lot of other kids are shy, too. If you can just be yourself, other people can relax and be themselves too!

Sometimes when you are nervous or scared, you behave in ways that you would not normally behave. My mom says she always demonstrates to others the person that she really is inside. She never puts on a fake personality.

She says that when you try to be someone you're not, you might end up making friends who don't really understand how you think and feel. Also, pretending to be different than you really are can make you feel bad about yourself. My mom always gives my sister and me great advice about life. The older I get, the more I realize that what she says is true.

We stayed in Toronto for only one year before my dad was transferred to a new office in Portland, Maine. By that time, I was nine and my sister was eleven. We were both excited to be returning to the United States. We couldn't wait to see what our new home would be like. My mom and dad knew a lot about Portland. They used to take trips there before my sister and I were born.

I decided to do a little research before we moved. I found a profile of the state in an atlas at home. Maine is a really cool state in northern New England. Portland is a small city on the Atlantic coast, but it has a lot to offer.

My mom and dad are really into nature and outdoor activities, so they were really looking forward to living in Maine. My dad said he couldn't wait to take us camping. He said, in the summer, we could go sailing and swimming at the beach. My sister and I were really excited about living in a place where there was so much to do.

On the first day at our new house in Portland, we were surprised to find that we already had visitors! While we were unpacking, my sister happened to look out the window. A family of deer was calmly chewing on grass in our backyard. We were so lucky to be able to see these animals up close. After that day, the deer came to visit us many more times. They were very good guests.

We've been living in Maine for three years now. Like the other times we moved, it was difficult adjusting to our new surroundings at first. Many of the kids who live here in Portland have lived in Maine their entire lives. As a result, it was a little bit harder for my sister and me to feel at home here. At first, we felt like outsiders because we had not grown up with all of the other kids.

We have spent a lot of time participating in outdoor activities here. We got the chance to go whale watching on a school field trip, and ever since then, I have been really interested in studying marine biology. I will always remember seeing a giant humpback whale swim by our boat. It was one of the most amazing experiences I've ever had.

Just a few weeks ago, my parents told my sister and me that we would be moving again. My dad was getting a promotion at work, and this meant that we were finally going to settle down in one place. Of course, my sister and I were sad because we did not want to leave our friends and home in Portland, but we also knew that we could handle the change.

Moving has taught me a lot about myself. Because of my experiences, I have become a much stronger and more independent person. I'm no longer afraid of meeting new people and seeing new places. In two weeks, we'll be moving back to Boston, and I will finally get a chance to ride those swan boats again.

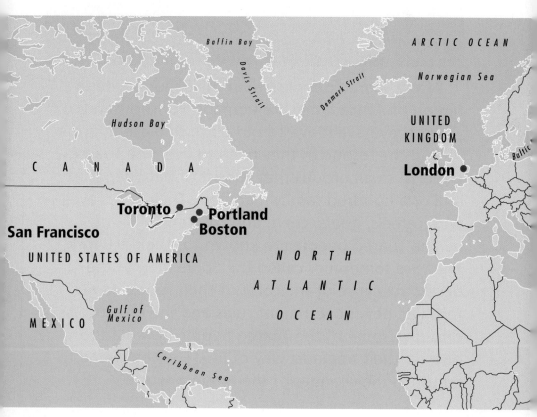

A Nomad's Life

Many Tuareg people live in the Sahara, a desert region of Africa. They are nomads. For thousands of years, they have moved from place to place in order to find the resources they need to live. The Tuareg travel in small groups that consist of between thirty and one hundred family members. They also travel with camels, goats, cows, and chickens.

The Tuareg people are known for their artwork. They are sometimes called the "blue men of the desert" because of the color of their robes. As a result of new government rules and the effects of drought, some of the Tuareg people have had to give up their nomadic way of life. They have had to adjust to the changes of the modern world.